21st Century Architecture

DESIGNER HOUSES

21st Century Architecture

DESIGNER HOUSES

images
Publishing

Published in Australia in 2012 by
The Images Publishing Group Pty Ltd
ABN 89 059 734 431
6 Bastow Place, Mulgrave, Victoria 3170, Australia
Tel: +61 3 9561 5544 Fax: +61 3 9561 4860
books@imagespublishing.com
www.imagespublishing.com

National Library of Australia Cataloguing-in-Publication entry:

Author: Mark Cleary.
Title: Designer houses / Mark Cleary.
ISBN: 9781864704419 (hbk.)
Series: 21st century architecture.
Subjects: Architecture, Modern.
               Architecture, Domestic.
               Interior decoration.
Dewey Number: 728

Edited by Mark Cleary/Debbie Ball

Designed by The Graphic Image Studio Pty Ltd, Mulgrave, Australia
www.tgis.com.au

Pre-publishing services by Mission Productions Limited, Hong Kong
Printed by Everbest Printing Co. Ltd., in Hong Kong/China on 150 gsm Quatro Silk
Matt paper

IMAGES has included on its website a page for special notices in relation to this and
our other publications. Please visit www.imagespublishing.com.

CONTENTS

Caramel Architekten

500M² LIVING ROOM
Rodaun, Austria

The owners of this house – a couple with one child and maybe more to come – dreamt of moving from their apartment in the middle of the city to a house in a more natural setting. They envisioned children playing in the grass while parents and friends watched on, and all around nothing but nature.

The site is a 500-square-metre grassy meadow dotted with trees. Consisting of four levels – three above ground and one below – the combined total living space is 300 square metres. In order to retain the character of the original meadow, the ground-floor living and dining areas are tied to the garden in a generous sweeping gesture. This gives the feeling of a 500-square-metre living room composed of outdoor and indoor spaces. The tail end of the 'swoosh' tapers to human scale, forming smooth, shallow depressions for sitting; curvilinear furniture; a pool and terrace with rounded corners.

Photography Hertha Hurnaus (www.hurnaus.com)

The 'sweeping gesture' on the ground floor is constructed of semi-transparent polycarbonate elements. The ephemeral character of the material is also employed in the top-floor façade, giving it the appearance of an airy, hovering swoosh. On the rooftop, the patch of meadow removed from below is woven into the undulating green office landscape.

1 Living
2 Closet
3 WC
4 Vestibule
5 Kitchen
6 Pool
7 Garden
8 Bedroom
9 Master bedroom
10 Walk-in-robe
11 Bathroom
12 Home office
13 Terrace

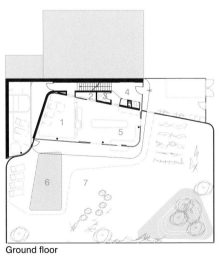

Ground floor

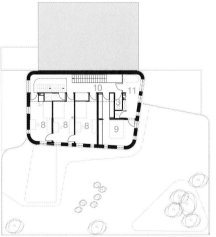

First floor

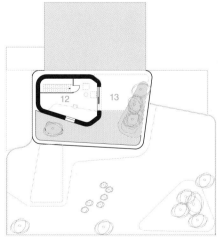

Second floor

Elsye Alam (id-ea)

ALAM FAMILY RESIDENCE
Jakarta, Indonesia

The open frontage of the Alam Family Residence contrasts with neighbouring houses, most of which are surrounded by large fences and contain guard booths. The highly articulated concrete wall acts as a 'breathing' brise-soleil, preventing overheating of the building skin and filtering abstract light patterns that transform the interior space throughout the day and night.

The roofscape geometry maximizes roof accessibility by connecting the second-storey to the third-storey portion of the house, culminating in a spectacular view of an historical marina to the east of the site. The roof deck serves as an alternative outdoor space for play and interaction, or simply a place to enjoy the sunrise, while the extensive rooftop garden contributes to the urban ecosystem.

The E-shape plan creates two inner voids that bring light and fresh air deep into the house. Generous use of skylights and extensive vertical glazing around the inner courtyards dispense with the need for artificial lighting during the day while creating a constantly-changing light display that activates and enlivens internal spaces.

Photography Fernando Gomulya

The interior of the house consists of a series of continuous, free-flowing spaces that foster a supportive, interactive family lifestyle. The consistent minimal white palette in the common area gives visual dominance to the bold red prayer niche – representing the family's traditional beliefs in a modern setting – the bold yellow aquarium located in the heart of the dining–living areas, the dark wood 'rolling carpet' of the staircase, the abstracted Borneo jungle water wall with native natural stone and the vertical garden in the courtyard.

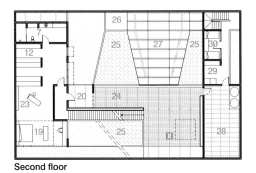

Second floor

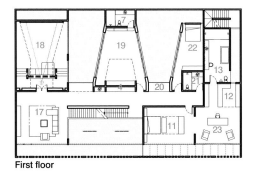

First floor

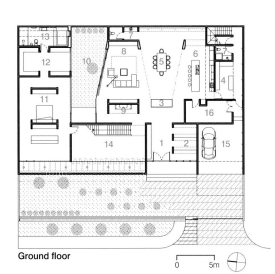

Ground floor

0   5m

1   Foyer
2   Shoe closet
3   Aquarium
4   Pantry
5   Dining
6   Kitchen
7   Bathroom
8   Living
9   Prayer room
10 Inner courtyard
11 Master bedroom
12 Walk-in robe
13 Master bathroom
14 Gallery
15 Carport
16 Storeroom
17 Family room
18 Home theatre
19 Bedroom
20 Balcony
21 Guest bathroom
22 Guest bedroom
23 Reading room
24 Roof deck
25 Roof garden
26 Mechanical roof
27 Skylight
28 Service area
29 Laundry
30 Maid's room

Humberto Hermeto Arquitetura

CASA JE
Nova Lima, Minas Gerais, Brazil

The challenge faced by the architect in this project was to create a large residence, with five bedrooms and generous living and leisure spaces, as well as a large gallery for the owner, an art enthusiast.

The irregular form and shape of the site, at first glance a complicating factor, ended up guiding the project, with the 10-metre slope leading to the decision to locate the residence and gallery on two separate levels.

The gallery occupies the lower level. With the need for an air-conditioned closed space, the volume arises from the ground like a big rock or platform.

The top level comprises the living quarters. Each room on this level is positioned to make the most of the impressive views – the mountain range can be seen from each room of the house. The 81-metre-long reinforced-concrete roof forms a portico over the front entrance, setting the residence's built volume.

Photography Jomar Bragança

Movement between the various levels of the residence is conducted via an elevator at the central core, directly connecting the first level of the gallery to the residence level. At an intermediate level, it connects the service and garage floor (and the mezzanine of the gallery).

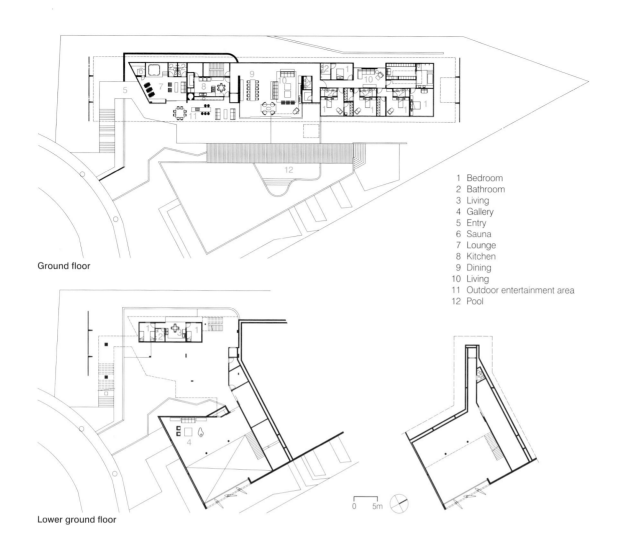

Ground floor

Lower ground floor

1 Bedroom
2 Bathroom
3 Living
4 Gallery
5 Entry
6 Sauna
7 Lounge
8 Kitchen
9 Dining
10 Living
11 Outdoor entertainment area
12 Pool

0   5m

Parque Humano

CASA SE
Léon, Guanajuato, Mexico

The most important determining factor of this project was the need for the design to accommodate the requirements of the owners' visually impaired son. The challenge was to generate a sensorial experience rooted in sounds and smells within a design that allowed for easy orientation and in which spaces were in direct contact with the outdoors.

The volume of the building responds to the movements of the sun and wind in order to create a comfortable internal environment without the need of mechanical systems. The main volume of the building contains the studio, the dining room/reflection pool, television room, and bedrooms. The intersecting volume comprises the living room, the dining room, and the kitchen.

Photography Paul Rivera (Arch Photo)

Geometry, structure, and construction were viewed as a single concept during the development of the project. The decision to use a structural system consisting of reinforced concrete slabs, which lend themselves to modular repetition, allowed for quick construction and lower costs.

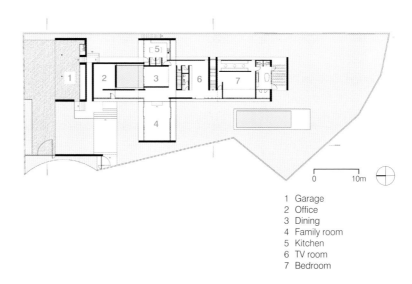

0   10m

1 Garage
2 Office
3 Dining
4 Family room
5 Kitchen
6 TV room
7 Bedroom

Balance Associates Architects

CORTES ISLAND RESIDENCE
Cortes Island, British Columbia, Canada

The clients for this project were looking for a house that would eventually become their full-time residence, but could also serve as a getaway, vacation and gathering place in the interim.

Located at the south end of Desolation Sound on Cortes Island, British Columbia, the site is formed of natural granite bedrock and contains a dramatic peninsula and cliff that serve as a windbreak for Cortes Bay, as well as the Seattle and Vancouver yacht clubs. To the south, the house is exposed to the Strait of Georgia, which delivers extremely high wind speeds and salt spray during winter storms. To withstand the high winds, the house structure is embedded in the bedrock with steel columns and exposed wood floor beams, allowing the house to cantilever off the hillside. Steel cross braces resist the large lateral forces brought by the high winds. The entry side of the house sits level with the bedrock and is made of concrete forms that create the entry space and visually anchor the house to the site.

Photography Steve Keating

From the entry, one accesses the central great room, including the living, dining and kitchen, all with expansive views to the strait beyond. The great room is flanked by a guest suite and study to the west. The master suite, which captures the morning sun, lies to the east.

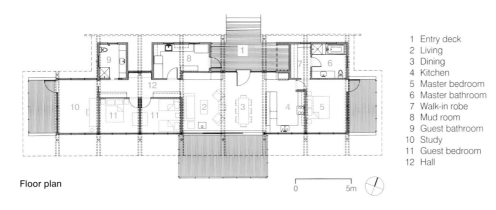

Floor plan

1 Entry deck
2 Living
3 Dining
4 Kitchen
5 Master bedroom
6 Master bathroom
7 Walk-in robe
8 Mud room
9 Guest bathroom
10 Study
11 Guest bedroom
12 Hall

0   5m

DAVIS RESIDENCE
Toronto, Ontario, Canada

Davis Residence is an exploration of the traditional division of a building into base, middle and roof. To accommodate the occupants' casual lifestyle, the architects developed an open floor plan on the ground floor, where the kitchen and family room are one and the same, opening up to the garden. A skylight filters soft light into the space and expansive sliding doors disappear to highlight the seamless integration of interior with the outside garden. There is an open flow from the kitchen–family room to the living room and dining room. The dining room has no doors, just views through the living room, through the fish tank and out to the garden.

The first-floor walls are free of the base in plan. The walls follow the profile of the soaring roof above and are finished in white plaster to reinforce the concept of lightness as the house lifts to the sky. The bedrooms are lifted up and away from the earth. The first floor has an open den at its heart. Three children's bedrooms and the master suite flow from it. The master suite, with its views towards the garden, catches the morning light. The first-floor exterior walls start to disappear as they rise towards the roof. The result is spaces with views to the densely wooded site, bringing the green forest inside. Trees on the perimeter of the site provide a privacy buffer with neighbours.

Photography Tom Arban

The swimming pool room is designed with doors that disappear into the walls connecting the exterior patios to the pool deck. The basement contains a full sports center, the focal point of which is a championship-size squash court, overlooked by an entertainment area and a sports bar.

Lower ground floor

Ground floor

First floor

1 Squash court	7 Electrical room	13 Laundry
2 Poll equipment	8 Mechanical room	14 Office
3 Change room	9 Sport room	15 Kitchen
4 Shower	10 Mud room	16 Breakfast room
5 Steam room	11 Garage	17 Patio
6 Media room	12 Bedroom	18 Family room

19 Dining	25 Walk-in robe
20 Entry	26 Gym
21 Living	27 Play room
22 Terrace	28 Master bathroom
23 Swimming pool	29 Master bedroom
24 Bathroom	

Alterstudio Architects, LLP

EAST WINDSOR HOUSE
Austin, Texas, USA

Extraordinary views in the heart of the city and a small buildable footprint limited by restrictive easements prompted a thin, three-storey home with the main living spaces and master suite on the top floor – essentially a one-bedroom loft with 270° views. A 40-centimetre ipe screen envelopes the body of the house, resting delicately atop a base of long courses of black Lueders limestone. The visitor enters through a pivoting glass door, where the natural stone gives way to its dressed counterpart, and is immediately greeted by a stair of massive ebonised oak treads floating above twin steel channels and hanging in a three-storey vertical space. Beyond, an etched glass wall captures the projected shadows of a stand of giant bamboo, and a band of clear glass directs one's gaze out to a private garden.

Punctuating the ipe façade are two steel box windows, their mirror-like reflection or deep shadow posed against the filigree of the screen. In the evening, this screen transforms into a lantern revealing a collection of spaces behind. The screen also holds the possibility of transforming the building when two 25-centimetre sections dramatically unfold and reveal the formal dining room.

Photography Paul Finkel

Upstairs, efforts are made to embrace the expansive view with an unmitigated ceiling plane that provides a surface for reflected light, while the screen's 45-centimetre extension above the floor level gently corrals the visitor. Adjacent power lines to the west are eschewed, although a constellation of portholes arrayed across this wall embrace the dramatic western light and enliven the façade from the high street beyond. Here, an open plan is accentuated by laminated low-e corner glazing, twin Akari lanterns and sliding panels. Exquisitely matched Lacewood veneer cabinetry and a marble bathing area punctuate the ensemble and add a sense of finesse and delicacy throughout.

Second floor

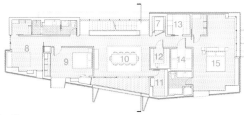

First floor

1 Entry
2 Library
3 Patio
4 Garage
5 Storage
6 Courtyard
7 Elevator
8 Exercise/Bedroom
9 Bedroom
10 Dining
11 Wine storage
12 Prep kitchen
13 Laundry
14 Mechanical room
15 Guest suite
16 Living
17 Deck
18 Kitchen
19 Pantry
20 Powder room
21 Master suite

Ground floor

0   3m

FOLD PLACE
Glebe, Ontario, Canada

The clients for this project requested open, flowing spaces in which simplicity would make modest dimensions seem bigger. Architect Andrew Reeves' response was a tight composition of volumes that maximizes the potential of the narrow, irregular-shaped site while still generating a singular street profile.

The street-side component of the two-storey core volume steps in to facilitate an eastern side entrance. A cantilevered bay wraps around the corner at the second level, its crisp lines, layering of planes and contrasting materials producing a piece of geometric art. On the opposite elevation, a single-storey garage, clad in richly stained pine in contrast to the neutral light-grey stucco of the main volume, is extruded on the angle of the lot.

Inside, an animated 'folding' of space creates horizontal and vertical fluidity and interconnectedness. The largely white walled and simply detailed interior rotates around two totemic elements centred on the west and east elevations of the house. One is a sculpted staircase whose ebony strained treads without risers seem almost to float. The other is a light chimney, a countering void marked by a soaring opaque window spilling light onto an interior garden at its foot. These elements also serve to separate the kitchen–dining area from the living room, but without impeding a sense of openness.

**Photography Erin Warder
(Eat and Breathe Photography)**

A generous and eclectic use of windows and glazed doors draws in light from all sides. If large picture windows that provide stunning tableaus of the Aberdeen's impressive cupola and the backyard facing wall glazed doors are boldly voyeuristic, many narrow vertical slot and horizontal clerestory windows contribute slices of views while protecting privacy.

In sum, Fold Place is an urban dwelling for an informal lifestyle that is committed to engaging its community with openness and sass.

Roof terrace

First floor

Ground floor

Basement

1 Garden
2 Entertainment room
3 Bathroom
4 Change room
5 Sauna
6 Mechanical room/Laundry
7 Kitchen
8 Dining
9 Interior garden
10 Entry
11 Social space
12 Powder room
13 Garage
14 Bedroom
15 Open to below
16 Master bedroom
17 Lounge
18 Rooftop patio

GARDEN PATIO
Kharkov, Ukraine

The character of the Garden Patio house is heavily influenced by the four gardens it interacts with. First is the city botanical garden, the green groves of which the house enjoys wonderful views. Second is the house's own sloping garden. Four elegant rectangular terraces mark the different levels, presenting a peculiar contrast with the natural landscape. The different orientation of the terraces creates a dynamic connection between the house and its surroundings. The terraces grow wider as they descend the hill, creating more usable space.

The third garden is a real secret garden — a cosy nook, shrouded in mystery and romance. Entrance to this chamber garden is only via the terrace formed by the difference in layers.

Photography Andrey Avdeekno

The fourth garden, the winter garden, is the 'green heart' of the house, situated at the very core of the multi-functional living space. Around the winter garden there is a sequence of zones, each having its own function: kitchen, dining, lounge, traditional Russian samovar display area, office and swimming pool. The members of the family can be in different zones, but at the same time stay in one single common space. Visual connections between all internal spaces intersect the layer of the winter garden with tropical plants. The winter garden also plays a major role in the gallery of the second floor, where the bedrooms are situated.

Ground floor

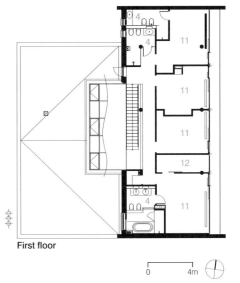
First floor

1 Terrace	7 Kitchen
2 Swimming pool	8 Living
3 Sauna	9 Study
4 Bathroom	10 Hall
5 Dining	11 Bedroom
6 Winter garden	12 Wardrobe

0   4m

Axis Architects

H-HOUSE
Salt Lake City, Utah, USA

The site of H-House is adjacent to the painted 'H' rock overlooking Salt Lake Valley, with the house positioned to take advantage of favourable southern and western views while being protected against the harsh afternoon sun.

The finished design approaches each of the programme elements, seamlessly integrating them into the overall built form. Designing the home to blend with the site's existing topography resulted in a final form consisting of three levels. The lower level contains a garage, storage space and an entrance foyer. All public areas are located on the main level – including the living–dining areas, kitchen and a cantilevered music room – and can be configured to create one large open space.

The master bedroom, which the client requested be contained on this level, maintains a physical separation from the public areas while accessing the most favorable views. These western views are central to the layout of the main level, indicated by the large exterior balcony near the living area. The upper level contains the home's remaining private spaces, including a study and two bedrooms.

The two main forms of the house are separated by a 'canyon' designed to allow for both vertical and horizontal ventilation. The corridor is naturally illuminated via skylights and serves to differentiate between major areas of the residence.

Photography Paul Richer (Richer Images)

Materials such as architectural concrete and Corten steel cladding were selected for the exterior because they require almost no routine maintenance and enhance the modern aesthetic of the house. The sophistication of the exterior is maintained in the interior finishes and details, combining to form a modern residential icon for Salt Lake City.

1 Garage
2 Vestibule
3 Family room
4 Dining
5 Kitchen
6 Deck
7 Master bedroom
8 Office
9 Study
10 Bedroom
11 Bathroom
12 Powder room
13 Laundry

Lower level

Main level

Upper level

0   3m

HEADLAND
North Curl Curl, New South Wales, Australia

Set on a sloping south-facing site, the Headland house hovers above one of Sydney's classically laidback Northern Beach suburbs. The beguiling nature of the setting masks what on closer scrutiny reveals a complexity of conditions that directly informed the architects' response in creating a relaxed and well-accommodated family home.

The ocean and the beach are to the southeast and the sweeping views out over the district to the south of the site culminate in views of the Sydney CBD skyline to the southwest. In addition to this, there is a nature reserve to the north.

Capturing all of these aspects became the focus and the challenge of the Headland house design. The lower level is cut firmly into the hill and kept intentionally solid (rendered masonry with clean-cut vertical slot openings). This level houses all the bedrooms, a large laundry, garaging, and a family room spilling out onto the back garden and swimming pool.

Photography Murray Fredericks and James Rice (Vision Photography)

The upper level, by contrast, is lightweight and serpentine, twisting and turning to maximize its aspect and capture all available views, drawing them into the house. This twist in the upper-level form sitting over the solid base (likened to a lizard on a rock) creates two distinct terraces on the flat roof of the lower level. These feed directly off the main living–dining room. This duality enables the residents to track the Australian sun (or avoid it if it gets too hot), and with large openings on opposite sides, establishes excellent natural cross-ventilation and shaded central living space.

This level comprises all the features expected in a large contemporary family house: a media room, a computer room-cum-study, plus the requisite open-plan kitchen, living and dining area. Raised two steps higher than the surrounding area, the kitchen commands an elevated aspect to the south and directly overlooks the pool and garden for optimum surveillance of the young ones.

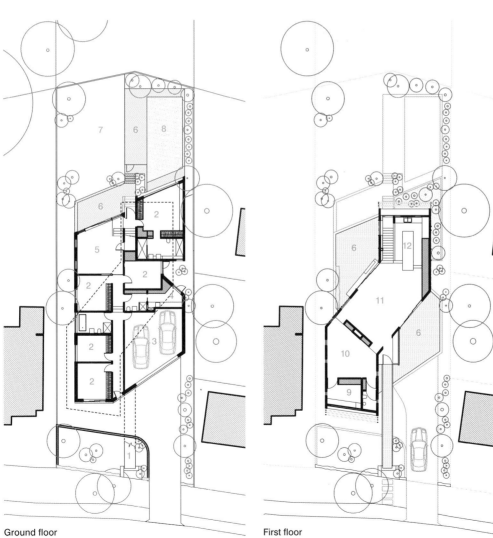

Ground floor

First floor

1 Bridge/Entry
2 Bedroom
3 Garage
4 Laundry
5 Rumpus room
6 Terrace
7 Garden
8 Pool
9 Study
10 Media room
11 Dining/Living
12 Kitchen

0   5m

McClean Design

HOLLYWOOD HILLS RESIDENCE
Los Angeles, California, USA

The new residence is a remodel of an existing home that was designed in the French style during the 1970s and was in very bad shape. The original structure was stripped down to framing and rebuilt in a contemporary style to take advantage of the magnificent views over the city of Los Angeles below.

Both the house and pool are L-shaped in configuration. Central to the design concept was the removal of the existing pool, which was located in the middle of the yard, and pushing out a new pool to the perimeter of the lot to produce a larger outdoor living space wrapped by the house and the infinity pool.

Ceiling heights were increased in the main living areas and the plan opened up to visually connect the different spaces. A key element of the design is the transparent sliding door systems that open the interior up to the outdoors and the view.

Photography Nick Springett

The house is laid out on one level, something of a rarity in the Hollywood Hills, and consists of three bedrooms in addition to the living, dining, kitchen and family room, as well as a small screening room or gym. The palette of materials was kept simple through the use of white limestone, brushed aluminum and stainless steel warmed by oak walls and cabinetry.

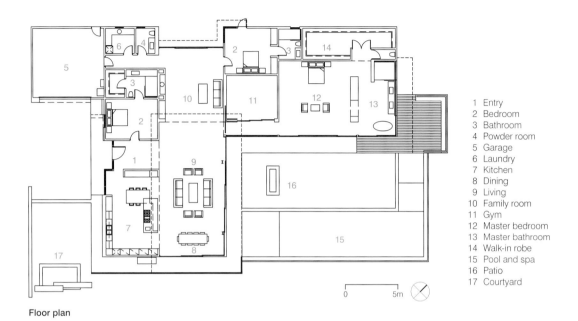

Floor plan

1 Entry
2 Bedroom
3 Bathroom
4 Powder room
5 Garage
6 Laundry
7 Kitchen
8 Dining
9 Living
10 Family room
11 Gym
12 Master bedroom
13 Master bathroom
14 Walk-in robe
15 Pool and spa
16 Patio
17 Courtyard

0   5m

HONITON HOUSE
Bellevue Hill, New South Wales, Australia

The architects approached the redesign of Honiton House as an opportunity to take a large compartmentalised house and open it up to create a contemporary flow that enabled the interior spaces to connect to exterior spaces over different levels. Landscape elements continue from garden to interior to emphasise seamlessness, while respecting the language of the original arts-and-crafts-style architecture.

A new orientation of key living spaces was a critical first step to maximising sunlight and natural ventilation. Connecting the formerly closed-off rooms was key to unlocking the home's spaces and bringing about highly usable and friendly living areas.

External and internal blinds, as well as sunshade awnings, were used to control exposure to the sunlight, while inside the house an open mezzanine has transformed the back hall into a functional focal point.

Photography Steve Back

The use of the large void to connect the kitchen, formal dining and living areas gives harmony to once disparate rooms. Light and the fine control of it further enhances the mezzanine, ensuring these spaces are inviting and useable at all times of the day.

The interior is kept neutral, with punches of colour used to add personality and character. All over the house the evocative contrast of intense textural materials is a striking design feature. Rough sandstone plays off against smooth concrete; timber screens contrast with lush plants; jewel-coloured tiles arranged in an Islamic fan pattern break up blocks of austere Calacatta marble.

A sandstone wall that 'snakes' its way through the building from inside to out is a clever tactical and visual device, used to connect a variety of spaces.

Lower ground floor

Ground floor

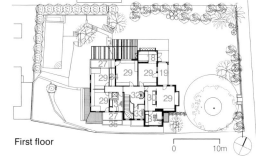

First floor

0   10m

1 Store
2 Garage
3 Cloak store
4 Informal lounge room
5 Wine cellar
6 Existing subfloor
7 Guest WC
8 Daybed
9 Pool
10 Spa
11 Upper courtyard
12 Lower courtyard

13 Existing entry
14 Existing foyer
15 Existing formal lounge
16 Existing powder room
17 Existing TV room
18 Existing sunroom
19 Existing terrace
20 Existing formal dining
21 New stair
22 Void
23 Dining courtyard
24 Kitchen

25 Study
26 Laundry
27 Terrace
28 Roof garden
29 Bedroom
30 Robe
31 Ensuite
32 Hallway
33 Bathroom
34 Linen
35 Planter

HORWITZ RESIDENCE
Venice, California, USA

The casually modern Horwitz Residence makes the most of the temperate Southern Californian climate by opening up to an outdoor living space that includes a pool, dining and barbecue area, and a play court. The simple, eco-conscious design is focused on functionality and the creation of a healthy family environment, with the interior/exterior courtyards, along with the master sliding window and living room sliders, allowing for optimum natural ventilation and maximum natural light.

Other passive sustainable elements include a solar chimney that draws in the cooler outside air and pushes out the warmer inside air during summer. The effectiveness of this simple design is such that a mechanical cooling system is not required. Further energy reductions are realized through the use of solar thermal radiant floor heating throughout.

Photography Art Gray

The architects made a conscious effort to use construction materials in their most organic form, and the contrasts of the various materials used (stone, steel, wood) add an element of warmth and family friendliness to this open and light contemporary home. Floor and ceiling materials are connected in an unobtrusive and whimsical manner to increase floor plan flow and space.

1 Courtyard
2 Lounge
3 Office
4 Master bedroom
5 Walk-in-robe
6 Ensuite
7 Powder room
8 Bathroom
9 Living/Dining
10 Kitchen
11 Pantry
12 Guest room
13 Verandah
14 Pool
15 Garage
16 Bedroom
17 Laundry

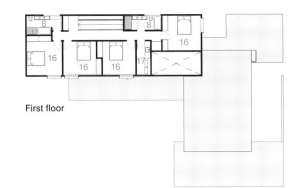

First floor

Ground floor

0   3m

HOUSE A + B
Santa Maria, Paros, Greece

House A+B consists of two holiday homes in one, designed to accommodate the needs of two families. The single volume is broken into a series of components that create a variety of niches, extrusions and spaces, achieving a plasticity of form yet at the same time architectural cohesion – both in the interior and the exterior – that reflects upon, respects and responds to the area's traditional Cycladic architecture.

The house is sited on a solid stone and concrete platform 80 centimetres above a preserved agricultural field immediately adjacent to the sea, giving dramatic views out to the bay, the sea beyond and the island of Naxos. The shifting layout allows the definition of several different outdoor spaces and rooms including breakfast terraces with outdoor kitchens, a dining terrace with a barbeque, and a terrace for watching movie projections at night. Inside, private spaces such as wet units and sleeping areas are accommodated in the separate family sections, while the 'public' living areas are accommodated in the 'in-between' zones as extensions of the outdoors.

Photography Dimitris Kalapodas

Designing for a holiday home in the Cyclades required sensible and sensitive strategies to take advantage of the area's particular environment and climate, which is generally defined by mild winters, year-round sunshine with a high intensity during the summer months, high average temperatures and a shortage of water, especially during the holiday season. The extensive translucent canopy acts as a vast climate moderator providing comfortable shaded areas for all-day use, especially during summer. Through efficient external insulation, the avoidance of direct sunlight hitting glazed surfaces and internal temperatures regulated via the foundation's thermal mass, the house remains comfortable through summer without the need for air conditioning or any mechanical cooling.

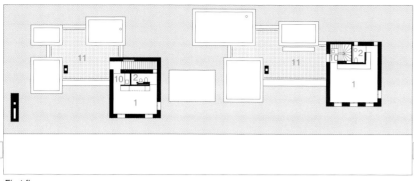

First floor

Ground floor

1 Master bedroom
2 Master bathroom
3 Living
4 Kitchen
5 Storage
6 Guest bathroom
7 Bedroom
8 Bathroom
9 Guest studio
10 Tea kitchen
11 Roof terrace
12 External shower
13 External kitchen
14 BBQ
15 Entry
16 Atrium/Night cinema
17 External living
18 Breakfast area
19 Play area
20 Sun deck

0   4m

Bento E Azevedo Arquitetos Associados

HOUSE CARQUEIJA
Camaçari, Bahia, Brazil

This site-sensitive single-storey house makes maximum use of space, emphasising outdoor living and providing functional and comfortable living areas. The simple, efficient plan includes a chapel and a large, flexible social area that integrates living, dining and a television room in an open space linked to the outside area via a porch.

The house is positioned horizontally on the site, with environmental concerns dictating the project work with the natural landscape and sloping topography, so that the house seems to float, creating two different levels of occupation. Steps from the porch lead to the garden, pool, barbecue and outdoor dining area.

Photography Tarso Figueira

For privacy, the house is closed off from front street views. Narrow windows and a brise-soleil on the west-facing front façade are designed to minimise solar gain, while the rear of the house completely integrates inside and outside through large windows, sliding doors and a porch, connecting the house with the green area.

As a result, at first contact the house appears as though a closed box. This first impression quickly dissipates upon entering, when one discovers ample open space bathed in natural light and strongly connected with the outdoors.

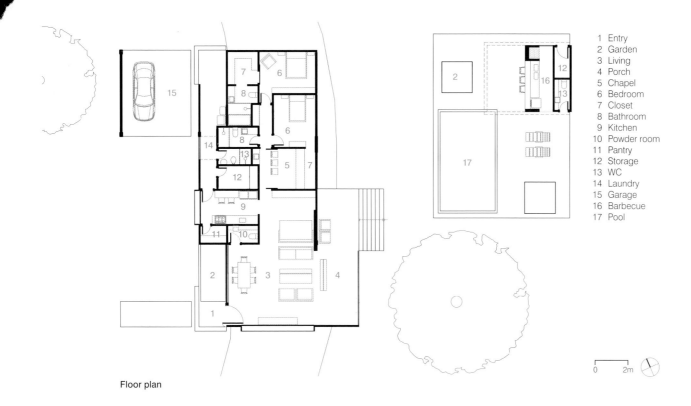

1	Entry
2	Garden
3	Living
4	Porch
5	Chapel
6	Bedroom
7	Closet
8	Bathroom
9	Kitchen
10	Powder room
11	Pantry
12	Storage
13	WC
14	Laundry
15	Garage
16	Barbecue
17	Pool

Floor plan

0   2m

Takashi Yamaguchi & Associates

HOUSE IN ISE
Ise, Japan

Located on a bluff surrounded by lush greenery and overlooking the beautiful Miyagawa River, House in Ise forms a rich relationship with its surroundings. The building is composed of two volumes running parallel to each other. A vertical void links the rooftop terrace and the light court on the ground floor, drawing nature into the interior. A horizontal void, located on the ground floor, connects directly to the vertical void and opens up views of Miyagawa River.

The ground floor of the eastern volume contains the living, dining and kitchen areas – all central to daily life. The dull sheen of the aluminium flooring gently amplifies the illumination from the light court and reflects the changing weather patterns onto the white interior throughout the day.

Photography Takashi Yamaguchi & Associates

The first floor contains family space and a bedroom in an enclosed area with a sloped ceiling. Milky-white natural light entering through slits in the roof creates a soft, subdued atmosphere.

A garage and study are located on the western volume's ground floor. The long, relatively low opening in the study enables eyes weary from reading to rest with a view of the abundant green landscape outside.

The rooftop terrace and light court are open to the surrounding natural beauty and afford excellent vantage points for the summer fireworks festival. The building's white exterior walls both reflect the fresh green of spring and catch the shadows cast by bare branches under the setting sun of late autumn. Such changing scenery is sure to create precious memories for the family that calls this house home.

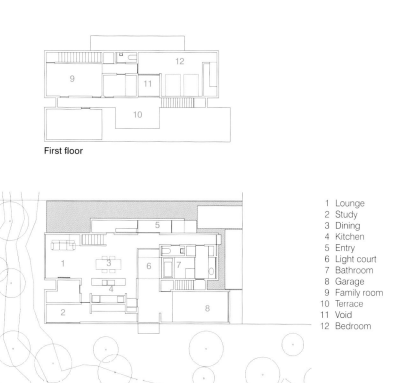

First floor

1 Lounge
2 Study
3 Dining
4 Kitchen
5 Entry
6 Light court
7 Bathroom
8 Garage
9 Family room
10 Terrace
11 Void
12 Bedroom

Ground floor

0   5m

HOUSE IN THE VILLAGE
Dalheim, Luxembourg

'Maison Mather' is a single-family house built to replace an old barn in Dalheim, a village 20 kilometres from Luxembourg. Working in the volume of the original barn, which butted up against another house, the design aims to remain modest and complementary to the 'art-deco-rural' style of the neighbouring house. The basement of the barn, with its vaulted cellar, was maintained as a platform for the new house. To accommodate the basement being 6 metres lower than the new house, a large terrace extending the living spaces and looking down onto the garden was incorporated into the plan.

The house is developed on three levels. The ground floor is a very open space that, from the street to the garden, gathers the social living areas: kitchen, dining and living room. Two children's bedrooms and one guest bedroom are contained on the garden side of the first floor, while the family room, to the street and southeast side, is the heart of the house. The more private parents' area, like a hotel suite, is located on the upper level. A large dormer volume gives generous space to the master bedroom and provides special views onto the garden.

Photography Christof Weber Photography

Clad in natural red cedar wood, the façade gives the appearance of a functional farm building in the local tradition. The entrance window and door are the same scale as the original barn gate in order to link the new design with the old. Wide use of shutters and sliding screens, other elements of the local rural architecture, make the street façade transformable, leaving the transparency of the house completely up to the inhabitants.

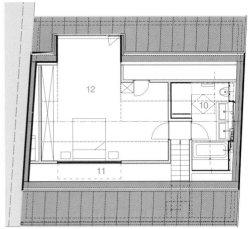

Second floor

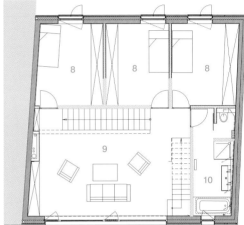

First floor

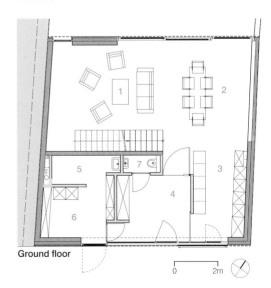

Ground floor

0   2m

1 Lounge   7 WC
2 Dining   8 Bedroom
3 Kitchen   9 Entertainment room
4 Hall   10 Bathroom
5 Technical room   11 Storage
6 Laundry   12 Master bedroom

HOUSE ON THE MOUNTAINSIDE

Ayora, Valencia, Spain

The sleek, clean lines of this white modernist house contrast starkly with the natural rugged mountain range from which it seems to shoot out like a kind of crystal from deep beneath the surface of the earth. Lined next to the more traditional houses in this small Spanish village, it appears alien, otherworldly, and yet at the same time perfectly suited to its surroundings.

The clean, minimalist aesthetic is continued indoors, where a central void divides the interior space. Located on the ground floor are the garage, wine cellar and laundry. The first floor contains two bedrooms, open to the private street, while a third bedroom on the second floor looks over the houses opposite and the Valley of Ayora. The study, also located on the second floor, opens onto to the central void, incorporating that space.

**Photography Fernando Alda
and Juan Rodríguez**

The open-plan living, dining and kitchen area on the second floor open onto an uncovered terrace that looks out to the rugged mountain range behind, making it a wonderful area for entertaining.

Architect; Fran Silvestre, Mª José Sáez
Interior Design; Alfaro Hofmann
Project team; Pedro Vicente López López, José Ángel Ruiz Millo,
José Vicente Miguel López, Fernando Usó Martin, Sara Sancho Ferreras

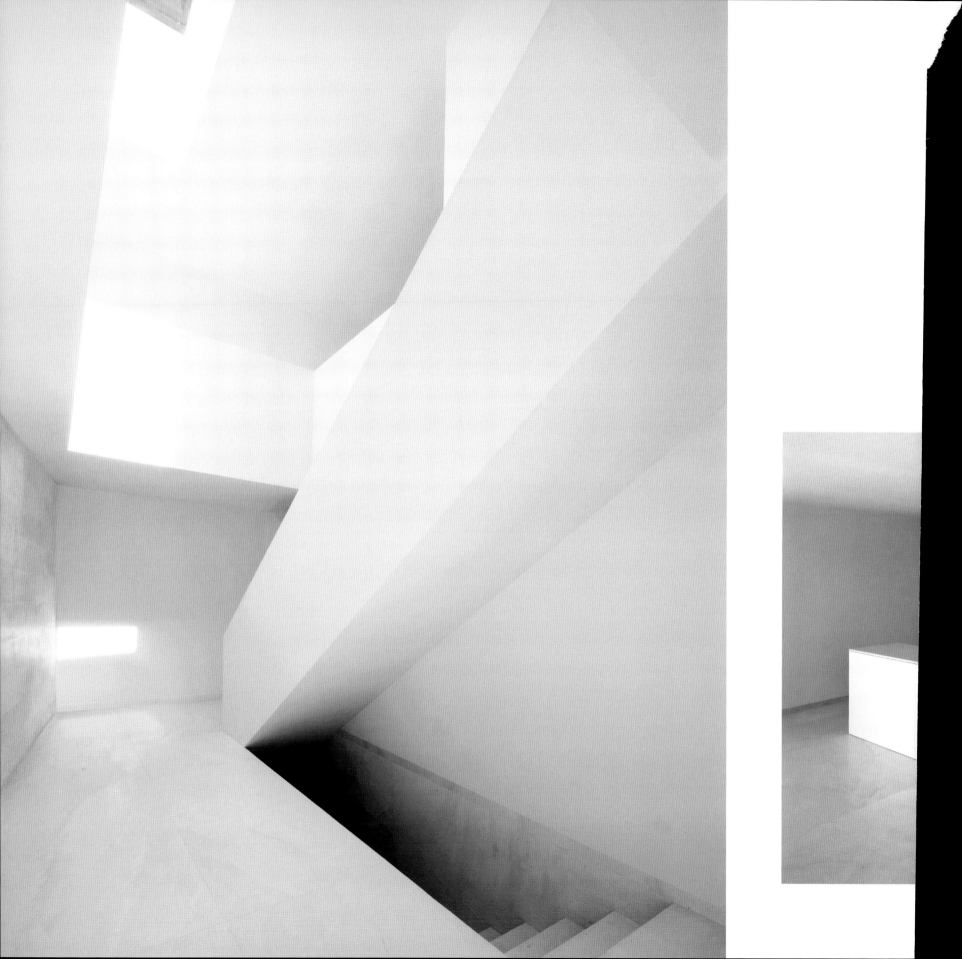

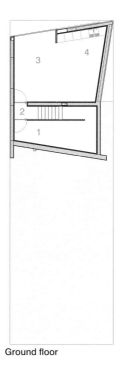
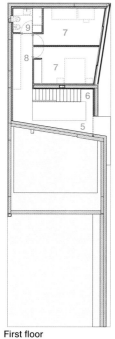

Ground floor

First floor

Second floor

1 Wine cellar
2 Vestibule
3 Garage
4 Laundry
5 Entrance hall
6 Staircase
7 Bedroom
8 Hall
9 Bathroom
10 Terrace
11 Lounge/Dining
12 Kitchen
13 Study

David Jameson Architect

KENSINGTON RESIDENCE
Washington DC, USA

Located 8 kilometres (5 miles) north of Washington DC, this house is a renovated residence for a young family situated amongst a subdivision of utilitarian post-war houses. The 685-square-metre (2250-square-foot) residence takes the form of a simple mass whose purity is interrupted by the void space of a carport. Bounded by an introverted exterior, luminous living spaces unfold in a series of interlocking volumes that are more urban and contained. Stairs become a series of intersecting diagonal slices through space. Cement-board sheets are sheared into abstract siding shingles that contribute to the unreadable scale of the building.

Photography Paul Warchol Photography

First floor

Mezzanine

1 Entry
2 Powder room
3 Kitchen
4 Dining
5 Living
6 Carport
7 Family room
8 Master bedroom
9 Master bathroom
10 Bathroom
11 Bedroom
12 Mechanical room

Ground floor

0   6m

95

Mojo Stumer

KINGS POINT RESIDENCE

Kings Point, New York, USA

The contemporary design of this modern retreat lends itself to the chic luxury one would expect from a suburban New York home. The design juxtaposes modern living with the preservation of the fantastic water views while suiting the homeowners' aesthetic bent.

The blue limestone, which runs the entirety of the lower level, enhances the soft, rich interior palette. Different finishes of absolute granite and high gloss wood lacquer were used to give texture and sheen to vertical surfaces. The clients' wide array of artwork was a key factor in the design, requiring vast open spaces, both inside and out, to display their extensive private collection.

Photography Scott Frances

Handcrafted millwork, custom windows and a double-height entry and living area give way to sprawling open areas, all of which are significant characteristics of the house. Outdoor entertaining areas are nestled in the tranquility of verdant landscaping, and the Long Island Sound serves as a picturesque backdrop.

Basement

Ground floor

First floor

1 Utility closet
2 Laundry
3 Training area
4 Wine cellar
5 Bathroom
6 Bar
7 Media room
8 Storage
9 Gym
10 Boiler room
11 Mechanical room
12 Garage
13 Office
14 Library
15 Foyer
16 Dining
17 Kitchen
18 Family room
19 Breakfast room
20 Pool bathroom
21 Bedroom
22 Walk-in-robe
23 Hall
24 Master bedroom

0   10m

Belzberg Architects

KONA RESIDENCE
Kona, Hawaii, USA

Nestled between cooled lava flows, the Kona residence situates its axis not with the linearity of the property, but rather with the axiality of predominant views available to the site. Within the dichotomy of natural elements and a geometric hardscape, the residence attempts to integrate both the surrounding views of volcanic mountain ranges to the east and ocean horizons to the west.

The programme is arranged as a series of pods distributed throughout the property, each having its own unique features and view. The pods are programmatically assigned as two sleeping pods with common areas, media room, master suite and main living space. An exterior gallery corridor becomes the organisational and focal feature for the entire house, connecting the two pods along a central axis.

To help maintain the environmental sensitivity of the house, two separate arrays of roof-mounted photovoltaic panels offset the residence energy usage, while the choice of darker lava stone helps heat the pool water via solar radiation. Rainwater collection and redirection to three drywells that replenish the aquifer are implemented throughout the property. The exterior of the home is constructed of reclaimed teak timber from old barns and train tracks. Coupled with stacked and cut lava rock, the two materials form a historically driven medium embedded in Hawaiian tradition.

**Photography Benny Chan (Fotoworks)
and Belzberg Architects**

Local basket weaving culture was the inspiration for the entry pavilion, which re-enacts the traditional 'gift upon arrival' ceremony. Various digitally sculpted wood ceilings and screens throughout the house continue the abstract approach to traditional Hawaiian wood carving, further infusing traditional elements into the contemporary arrangement.

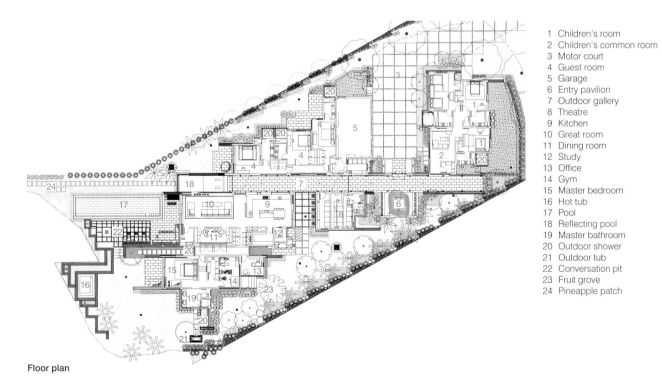

Floor plan

1 Children's room
2 Children's common room
3 Motor court
4 Guest room
5 Garage
6 Entry pavilion
7 Outdoor gallery
8 Theatre
9 Kitchen
10 Great room
11 Dining room
12 Study
13 Office
14 Gym
15 Master bedroom
16 Hot tub
17 Pool
18 Reflecting pool
19 Master bathroom
20 Outdoor shower
21 Outdoor tub
22 Conversation pit
23 Fruit grove
24 Pineapple patch

LAKEWOOD HOUSE
Northeastern USA

Set in a pine forest near a still lake, this rustic house stages a friendly argument between the built and the natural worlds, playfully mimicking nature while taking advantage of her benevolent charms. Fanning out like a heliotropic spring fern, the house follows the sun's daily arc, opening southward toward the water so inhabitants can closely observe and engage the outdoors with all their senses.

Connected shed roofs facing south provide deep overhangs to shade porches with tall columns that support a solar screen of indigenous logs. These rhythmically placed natural shades invite the sun's warming winter rays, but keep the house cool in summer. The roofs shoulder against north winds, while scattered leaf-like dormers lift skyward, luring daylight deep into the interior. The first floor flows seamlessly into the outdoors and onto a sitting porch through folding glass walls that open from side to side, merging interior and exterior into one great living space.

Photography Peter Aaron (Esto)

Inside, the main house is united by an arcing two-storey hall that doubles as a grand entry. Lined with walls made from local stones at the first floor, it has a catwalk balcony above leading to bedrooms and a studio. The hall serves as the main street for the house, connecting the garage and service rooms with the kitchen and the living room.

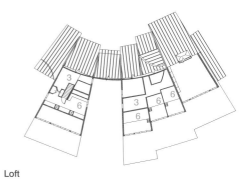

Loft

First floor

Ground floor

Lower ground floor

1 Media room
2 Games room
3 Mechanical room
4 Wine cellar
5 Powder room
6 Storage
7 Tractor garage
8 Mudroom/Laundry
9 Garage
10 Outdoor cooking area
11 Dining
12 Entry hall
13 Office
14 Music/Library
15 Kitchen
16 Living
17 Studio
18 Master bathroom
19 Master bedroom
20 Bathroom
21 Bedroom
22 Open to below

0   22ft

Jyrki Tasa

MOBY DICK HOUSE
Espoo, Finland

This biomorphic house peeks out onto the street from behind the rocks. A stair built of stone and a bridge out of steel lead to the main entrance on the first floor above ground level. One enters the building through a white organic outer wall. Located on this floor are the living room, library, master bedroom and two balconies. The ground floor houses children's spaces, a guestroom and a garage. The basement contains sauna facilities, a fireplace and a gym.

Floors are connected by a tall staircase as well as by a two-storey-high winter garden. Three translucent glass–steel bridges join these spaces as well. The staircase, which forms the spatial core of the house, is lit by a large skylight. From the staircase one has a view of the house from every direction – either directly or through diverse glass walls.

Photography Jussi Tiainen

The organic-shaped ceiling in the first floor complements free-form spatial organisation emphasised by the curved white outer wall. All interior walls are rectangular in section as opposed to the outer shell, which forms a dynamic contrast between the two. The house opens towards the southwest – in the direction of the garden – through large windows.

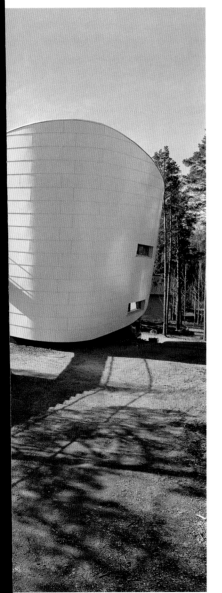

First floor

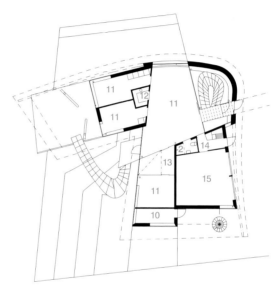

Ground floor

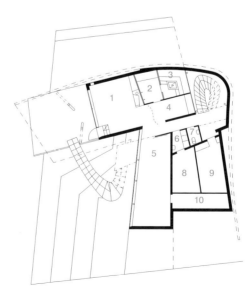

Lower ground floor

1 Sauna cabinet
2 Bathroom
3 Sauna
4 Dressing room
5 Gym
6 Cleaning room
7 WC
8 Technical equipment
9 Wine cellar
10 Storage
11 Bedroom
12 Clothes storage
13 Winter garden
14 Hall
15 Garage
16 Terrace
17 Study
18 Living
19 Wardrobe
20 Kitchen
21 Utility room
22 Balcony

Yasutaka Yoshimura Architects

NOWHERE BUT SAJIMA
Yokosuka, Kanagawa, Japan

This holiday rental home located on the central east coast of Japan, sited on a point of reclaimed land in a small fishing village, is a triangular block composed of tube-like volumes positioned towards the ocean. While the site meets the seawall and directly faces the sea, it also offers views of the buildings that line the coast.

To provide adequate privacy without the use of curtains, narrow tube-shaped spaces are bundled together and angled to provide openings toward the sea. The orientation of these tubes naturally blocks the line of sight from the adjacent apartments, and while gazing down the length of the tube from inside only the ocean can be seen.

Photography Chiaki Yasukawa and Yasutaka Yoshimura

While providing an escape from the tide of urbanism characterising what we normally call a 'resort', Nowhere but Sajima still maintains the key aspects of the resort experience. In this house the architects have managed to replicate the experience of looking out to sea from the deck of a ship.

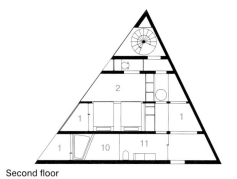

Second floor

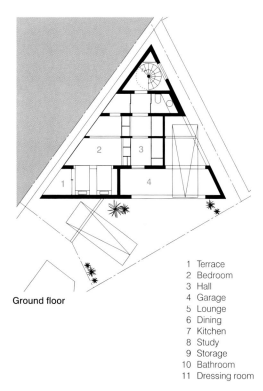

First floor

Ground floor

1 Terrace
2 Bedroom
3 Hall
4 Garage
5 Lounge
6 Dining
7 Kitchen
8 Study
9 Storage
10 Bathroom
11 Dressing room

Feldman Architecture

PACIFIC HEIGHTS TOWNHOUSE
San Francisco, California, USA

The Pacific Heights Townhouse is an update and reconfiguration of a 1906 stucco-clad Victorian house. The owners wanted to maintain the building's traditional feel, but also to infuse some modern elements, so the house would be both more livable and reflective of their personalities. They also wanted a light-filled house that would incorporate sustainable elements. Furthermore, the original house took up nearly the entire length of its lot and the clients wanted a garden that would be accessible from the main living spaces.

To achieve these goals, the architects placed the living areas on the top floor, where the light would be best and where, by removing a large portion of the rear space, a roof garden could be created. Most of the walls were removed from this floor to create spaces that are visually connected, yet functionally separate.

The building is set off the south property line, which allowed the addition of numerous large windows along the length of the house. New skylights on the north side flood the interior of the top floor and the long hallway on the second floor with natural light. Open-riser stairs, a light well, and interior windows also allow light to filter down to the second floor hall.

Photography Paul Dyer

Throughout the house modern elements are combined with the traditional in an unexpected manner. For example, a steel and glass staircase and garden wall, modern lighting, wallpaper, tile and cabinetry are set against traditional wainscoting, trim, and rustic wooden floorboards.

Significant sustainable elements were also incorporated into the design, including a solar-powered radiant heat system and a large photovoltaic roof array.

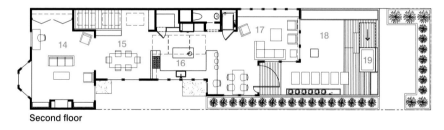
Second floor

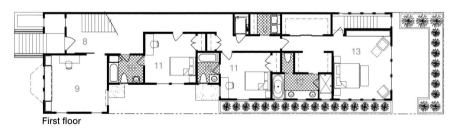
First floor

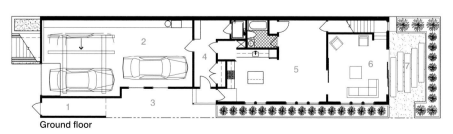
Ground floor

1 Side entry
2 Garage
3 Side yard
4 Lobby
5 Guest suite
6 Living area
7 Rear yard
8 Entry
9 Play room
10 Bathroom
11 Bedroom
12 Master bathroom
13 Master bedroom
14 Living
15 Dining
16 Kitchen
17 Family room
18 Roof garden
19 Spa

0   5m

PICTURE HOUSE
Ripatransone, Italy

The exterior of the Picture House speaks the language of the landscape that surrounds it, blending in with the natural environment, reflecting rural traditions and earthy colours.

Inside, the house becomes abstract, with the outside viewed through windows that appear as pictures on the walls. Every functional point of the house has one of these 'pictures' to view. The windows attract the landscape, framing it and projecting it inside.

The staircase seems to extend an invitation for exploration and discovery. It is an extension of the living room — a place to sit, to climb, to explore — an object of interest in itself, with its steps of varying size, its landing and ramps. The staircase extends to the outside terrace, creating a sense of continuity between inside and outside; and between ground floor, mezzanine and first floor. That the same material is used for the stairs, terrace and internal floor adds to this continuity.

Photography Fabio Barilari

The 'pictures' in the Picture House do not remain static: the colours, light and landscape changing with the day and with the seasons, captivating those inside with these natural moving images of beauty.

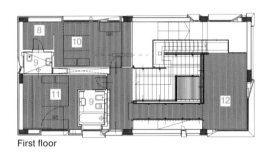

First floor

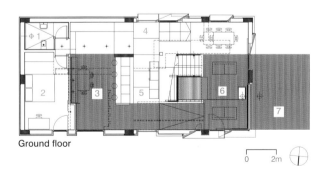

Ground floor

0   2m

1 Guest bathroom
2 Guest bedroom
3 Dining
4 Entrance
5 Kitchen
6 Living
7 Patio
8 Wardrobe
9 Bathroom
10 Master bedroom
11 Family bedroom
12 Mezzanine/Living/Studio

PINISI HOUSE
Jakarta, Indonesia

Pinisi House is situated within a small residential complex in Jakarta. In this development, privacy is a key essential ingredient. Right from the point of entry the house is seamlessly designed, managing to maintain privacy while at the same time allowing a good mix of both natural lighting and cross ventilation.

The main living space is elevated so as to avoid the direct view of the traffic along the slip roads to the estate. With the main spaces elevated to a new plane, the edgeless pool thus becomes the main focus, where the building gravitates. A luscious tropical landscape envelops the sides of the pool, with the planting of a 50-year-old tree completing the setting.

Each interlocking space creates a new realm of experience, making the most of the opportunities afforded by the tropical climate, integrating gardens and air wells to capitalise on the *genius loci*, or 'spirit of place'.

Photography Genius Loci

To complete the identity of the house, a uniquely patterned metal sunscreen plotted along the sun's path enables optimun solar deflection. Inspiration for the design was drawn from the basic forms of DNA code, translated into a graphic form. This identity tops off the playfulness of the house.

Architect/Designer Mr Alex Bayusaputro and Mr Stanley Savio (Genius Loci)
Main Contractor Mr Eka Hendrawan (PT Duta Kreasindo)
Lighting Consultant Hadi Komara

Second floor

First floor

Ground floor

1 Pump and
  genset
2 Driver's room
3 Laundry
4 Garden
5 Garage
6 Storage
7 Maid's room
8 Kitchen
9 Bathroom
10 Pump room
11 Home theatre
12 Carport
13 Balancing tank
14 Secret room
15 Foyer
16 Walk-in-robe
17 Dining room
18 Pantry
19 Master
   bedroom
20 Courtyard
21 Living
22 Foyer
23 Pond
24 Bedroom
25 Sitting room

0   5m

PRYOR RESIDENCE
Montauk, New York, USA

The Pryor Residence is sited atop a small hill, with views of the ocean in the distance. The design of the house prompts the owners to interact with the surrounding environment, evoking experiences of camping.

A departure from typical residential planning, the house has multiple entrances designed for different guests and for different occasions. Large glass doors slide open to the living, dining and kitchen areas for a large gathering; a smaller scaled swing door for an occasional guest opens to the centre hall with a view of the ocean; and a sequence of auxiliary spaces – beach equipment area, outdoor shower, and sand and mudroom – create a seamless ritual from the daily activities for the family and friends.

In all living areas and bedrooms, glass doors and insect screens slide in and out from pockets in the walls, transforming rooms to screened porches or spaces completely open to the landscape.

Photography Bates Masi Architects

The living area, a double-height space with kitchen, dining and living areas, has 36-foot-wide (11-metre) glass doors that pocket into southern and northern walls. When open, the dining room becomes a picnic area and the living room fireplace becomes a campfire. Multiple layers of bronzed metal fabric at the clerestory windows in the living area fold and unfold to adjust sunlight for optimal brightness and temperature.

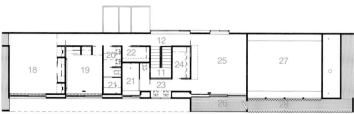

First floor

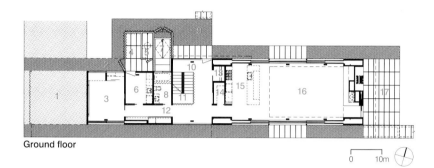

Ground floor

0   10m

1 Carport
2 Service entry
3 Guestroom
4 Storage
5 Outdoor shower
6 Mudroom
7 Basement entry
8 Guest bathroom
9 Entry patio
10 Entry hall
11 Stair
12 Hall
13 Coat closet
14 Pantry
15 Kitchen
16 Living/Dining
17 Patio
18 Kid's bedroom
19 Guest bedroom
20 Bathroom
21 Shower
22 Linen closet
23 Master bathroom
24 Master closet
25 Master bedroom
26 Balcony
27 Living/Dining below
28 Bris Soleil

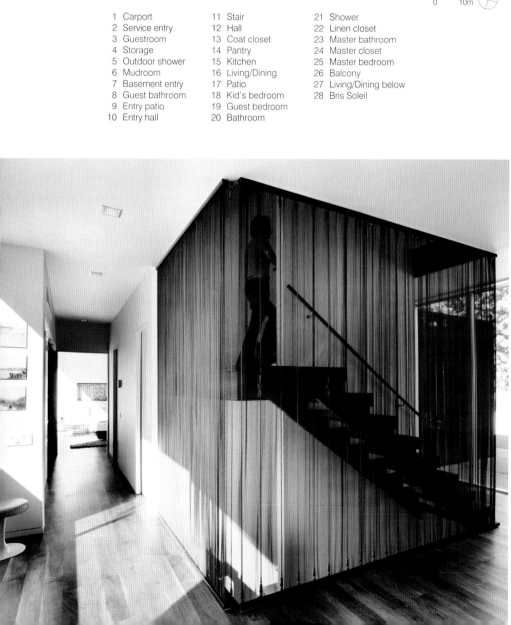

CplusC

QUEENS PARK RESIDENCE
Queens Park, New South Wales, Australia

Located in a noisy urban context – on the corner of a busy arterial road and laneway – an existing dwelling provided the setting for this significant transformation. The original masonry walls on the eastern and western façades were retained and recycled, in addition to the southern entry. The existing kitchen and living spaces were extended and the existing walls to the north were removed to make way for large glazed doors leading out to the new outdoor dining/terrace and pool areas.

The interior planning was dramatically re-worked to arrange the spaces around the ordering elements of the entry hall and service corridor. The new entry hall provides a warm circulation path, distinctly articulated in timber that branches into and connects the various spaces of the home.

Photography Murray Fredericks

The overall spatial concept is inspired by the experience of sheltering in the dappled light under the canopy of the Morton Bay figs in adjacent Centennial Park. Integral to the design of the house, and carried forward from the site's original structure, is the entry sequence, marked with a custom-designed recycled-jarrah door. Passing through this portal, the hallway extends through the house as an ordering element conceived as a tree trunk from which the private spaces of the home branch and around which the butterfly roof form is mirrored.

1   Entry
2   Hall
3   Master bedroom
4   Ensuite
5   Walk-in-robe
6   Kitchen
7   Lounge/Dining
8   Outdoor living
9   Pool deck
10 Pool
11 Bedroom/Study
12 Bathroom
13 Bedroom
14 Garage
15 Storage
16 Laundry
17 Pantry

0   3m

Ground floor

Thomas Elliott, Paramita Abirama Istasadhya (PAI)

RESIDENCE AT PRAPANCA
Jakarta, Indonesia

A lot of passion went into the design of Residence at Prapanca. The architectural style is neither classic nor modern, rather a combination of both, while the interior design has a modern, artistic aesthetic.

Each room is equipped with multiple openings, allowing natural light to shower in and brighten the interior while at the same time opening up views to the surrounding garden. Each bathroom also has an outdoor/indoor configuration.

Large natural teakwood doors and a dark marble floor make for an impressive entrance to the formal living, formal dining and reading room. A corridor leading to family areas displays an impressive collection of modern custom artwork of golden anodised aluminum by local artist Rita Widagdo. A clear separation between formal areas and family areas is a response to the needs of entertaining.

Photography Ibham Jasin

The dramatic open sitting room and terrace leading off from the family sitting room create a calming and relaxing space overlooking the swimming pool.

The master bedroom, with its large wardrobe surrounding an orchid courtyard, provides a totally different experience. A generous bathroom complete with his and hers shower and toilet plus sunken bathtub with glass skylight surrounded by an enclosed garden creates a sense of warmth and luxury.

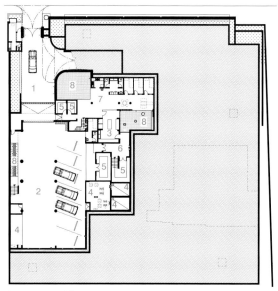

Lower ground floor

Ground floor

First floor

1	Driveway	9	Portico	17	Pantry
2	Garage	10	Foyer	18	Breakfast
3	Laundry	11	Living	19	Family room
4	Mechanical room	12	Formal dining	20	Terrace
5	Storage	13	Corridor	21	Entertainment room
6	Lobby	14	Reading room	22	Study
7	Maid's quarters	15	Prayer room	23	Powder room
8	Reflecting pond	16	Kitchen	24	Gym

25	Master bedroom	33	Hall
26	Wardrobe	34	Collection room
27	Master bathroom	35	WC
28	Children's bedroom	36	Guest bedroom
29	Children's wardrobe	37	Guest bathroom
30	Children's bathroom		
31	Swimming pool		
32	Garden		

0   5m

RICHMOND HOUSE
Richmond, Victoria, Australia

Responding boldly to the challenges of a tight inner city site, architect Michael Morris has provided a sanctuary amidst the traffic and intensity of the immediate surroundings. The interior is private, quiet and visually exciting. The exterior is assertive in its presence, yet not dominating and contributes to the vitality and interest of the street.

The front façade is notched to provide a protected entry and enable views of the adjacent Victorian cottage. Large screens prevent invasive views, and rooms revolve around protective courtyards and decks. An adjacent peppercorn tree also forms a protective veil. The established lush gardens are watered by rainwater tanks concealed behind a stacked stone wall along the entry path, which also holds grasses and orchids along the entry.

Photography Christopher Ott and Shania Shegedyn

The simple rectilinear form of the house creates spaces which flow into each other. The subtle palette of materials is deliberately restrained, relying on layering and transparency to create a sense of elusiveness. External finishes penetrate into the building and are highlighted by the selective use of interior colours and finishes. All 'Isobar' and 'Monsoon' tapware used in the building has been designed by the architect.

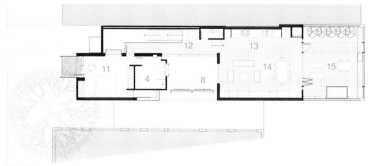

First floor

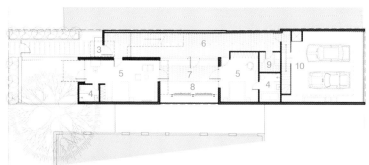

Ground floor

Lower ground floor

0   5m

1 Storage	6 Gallery	11 Master bedroom
2 Wine cellar	7 Courtyard	12 Upper gallery
3 Entry	8 Greenwall	13 Kitchen
4 Ensuite	9 Laundry	14 Living/Dining
5 Bedroom	10 Garage	15 Deck

Saaj Design / Willstruct Pty Ltd (Builder)

SOUTH YARRA HOUSE
South Yarra, Victoria, Australia

Responding to the site, a modest wedge-shaped suburban block, the strategy for the South Yarra House was to locate all primary living areas on the first floor to capture distant views and natural solar gain, while preserving privacy from nearby neighbours. The house façade addresses the street by adopting an orthogonal language to integrate it into the heritage street setting. As you move through the site the building form gradually starts to spread and cantilever like the canopy of a tree, flowing into a series of graceful arcs, sweeps and curves.

The framed, cantilevered façade has been formed by thousands of vertically laminated sheets of glass. The result is an abstract 'botanical' frozen waterfall. The entire wall responds internally to the ever-changing external light conditions, and at night glows outwards.

Photography Matthew Mallet, Patrick Redmond and Shania Shegedyn

The entire house is connected architecturally through circulation – via a 'spine' wall that starts off outside of the house. This wall progressively increases in scale as it slides under the mass of the upper levels. On the lower levels, sculpted joinery units are hung off and carved into the wall, which then grows into a cylindrical lift shaft and flows around a spiral, ribbon-like staircase. It culminates on the upper level, encasing a kitchen pod and a powder room that anchors the entire first floor living. The kitchen has the capacity to be concealed via curved metallic sliding doors, challenging our perception of what the kitchen is.

The bedroom zones, tucked below, reference the Marion Hall/Art Deco influenced interior of the original house.

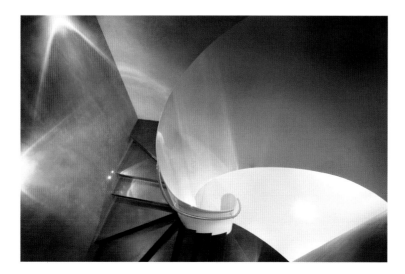

STONEHAWKE
The Gap, Queensland, Australia

The steep, difficult site is wedged into the side of a hill and nestled into a large parcel of heavily wooded environmentally protected land. The charred box protrudes horizontally like fallen lumber. Solidly grounded into the site, the body of the house wraps itself around an above-ground off-form concrete pool that also reflects the charred timber in its internal finish.

Raw and organic materials were used to blend with the natural surrounds of sandstone rockwork and various species of native tall trees. With this language, the cladding and structure are represented accordingly with rough sawn stained plywood, galvanised steel, and combinations of horizontal and vertical sections mimicking the tree forms.

From this point it was critical to both soften and refine the palette to the interior detailing while being mindful of the importance of the cohesion and notion of interior to exterior. Once formally inside, the occupants are transferred both visually and physically between this notion as the house opens up with counterbalanced glazing systems and sliding external glass walls.

Photography Christopher Frederick Jones

A central entry from the garage leads to the first-level entry point and voided space that leads either off to the parents' retreat or, further ascending, to the centre of the main body of the house. Although from the street it appears to be a three-storey house, 90 per cent of the programme is confined to the top level, which happens to be level with natural ground due to the slope of the site.

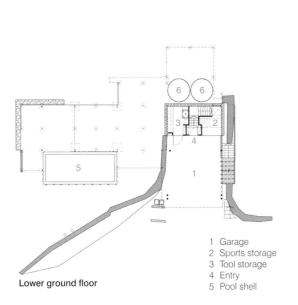

Lower ground floor

Ground floor

First floor

1 Garage	6 Water tank	11 Bedroom	16 Laundry	21 Kitchen
2 Sports storage	7 External entry	12 Private deck	17 Dining	22 Rumpus room
3 Tool storage	8 Internal entry foyer	13 Study/Sewing room	18 Living	23 Pool
4 Entry	9 Walk-in-robe	14 Bathroom	19 Deck 1	
5 Pool shell	10 Ensuite	15 Guestroom	20 Deck 2	

SUMAR BEACH HOUSE
Whangapoua, Coromandel, New Zealand

The brief for this project was for a collection of spaces that would open up in the summer and provide multiple outdoor living areas or act as a private sanctuary when used as a winter retreat.

The holiday home is of a typical residential scale and proportion. The main living quarters spans the width of the site, defining the road front and private backyard. The structures are intersected by a walkway that links the front entrance through the house to the private, north-facing living areas. It also connects the detached guests' quarters with the main living areas.

The walkway is defined with a solid canopy to the exterior and juxtaposed with a long glazed roof light that opens up the heart of the home. This is all tied together with a timber slatted boardwalk under the roof elements. The roof plane is penetrated by another two features that allow the spaces to experience the elements in a controlled manner.

Photography Jim Janse

The kitchen and bathroom share an internal screened garden, while the outdoor living pavilion links the two living wings by providing a gathering point that they can spill out onto.

The careful selection of timber accents and shell aggregate embedded within the honed concrete floor emphasise the link between the beach and the inner sanctuary of the holiday home.

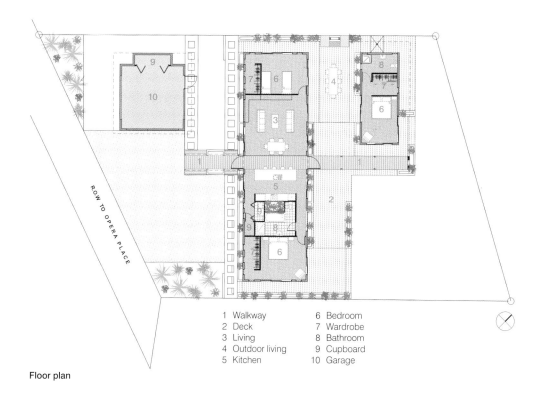

1 Walkway
2 Deck
3 Living
4 Outdoor living
5 Kitchen
6 Bedroom
7 Wardrobe
8 Bathroom
9 Cupboard
10 Garage

Floor plan

Jarmund/Vigsnæs AS Arkitekter MNAL

SUMMER HOUSE VESTFOLD
Vestfold, Norway

The Summer House is located on the coast of Vestfold, in the southern part of Norway, replacing an older building that formerly occupied the site. To secure the planning permit, the project had to be well adjusted to the terrain, in terms of shape, scale, material and colour.

The house and terraces are partly built upon existing stone walls. The newly constructed parts of the wall are made from stones resulting from blasting at the site.

Photography Nils Petter Dale

The low, elongated volume is cut in two to allow for wind-shielded outdoor areas, embraced by the house itself. These cuts also bring down the scale of the building and, together with the local variations of the section, make the building relate to the surrounding cliff formations.

On the outer perimeter of terraces and pool, a glass fence protects against wind while also allowing for maximum views. The Kebony wood cladding is treated via a sustainable process to make it more durable against exposure to the salt water.

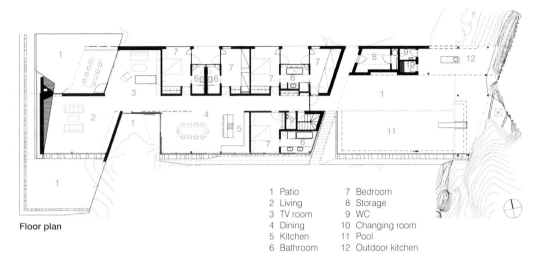

Floor plan

1 Patio
2 Living
3 TV room
4 Dining
5 Kitchen
6 Bathroom
7 Bedroom
8 Storage
9 WC
10 Changing room
11 Pool
12 Outdoor kitchen

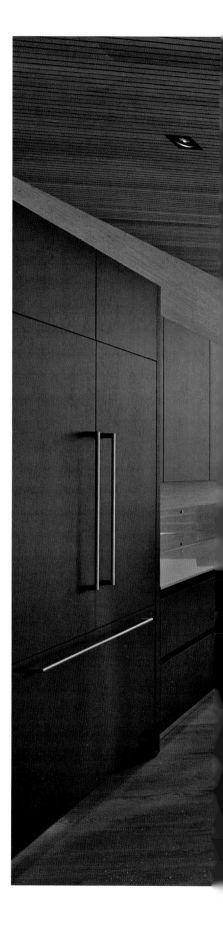

Connor + Solomon

SURFSIDE HOUSE
Clovelly, New South Wales, Australia

A timber platform extends across two-thirds of this beachside site, sheltered to the west by a three-storey stair spine, and to the east by a dense charcoal concrete block wall. Dividing the north-facing exterior deck and 12.5-metre lap pool from the interior are sliding and folding glazed doors, with summer shading provided by the large eaves of the undulating wall and library.

Where wall planes become a continuously wrapping enclosure, a quietening down of the environment and increased intimacy are achieved by the judicial placement of window openings and the selection of finer materials, such as natural timber veneers and fabric. This occurs also on the upper and lower sleeping levels, with the upper main bedroom opening up onto its own skyline terrace and the lower children's bedrooms opening out onto lawn and garden.

Photography Kraig Carlstrom Photography

Both builder and architect share a great passion for timber boat building, and the detailing of this house reflects the sensitivity and delicacy yet inherent longevity and robustness of timber boat design, utilising a joint understanding of Australian hardwoods, recycled timber and plantation-grown plywood.

1 Grey water recycling
2 Bathroom
3 Media room
4 Laundry
5 Stairs
6 Outside stairs
7 Bedroom
8 Drying area
9 Terrace
10 Lawn
11 Gym
12 Pool
13 Living
14 Shower room
15 Dining
16 Kitchen
17 Library/Informal living
18 Carparking deck
19 Entry
20 Ensuite
21 Robe and study
22 Master bedroom
23 Bedroom terrace
24 Storage
25 Roof terrace

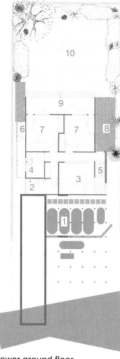

Lower ground floor

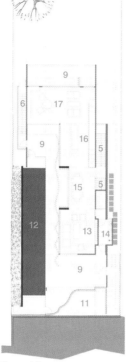

Ground floor

Upper ground floor

Roof terrace floor

0   5m

TAKAPUNA HOUSE
Takapuna, New Zealand

This project is a renovation of a 1980s architect-designed home. The existing architecture had an elegant structure comprising solid banks of bagged brick walls counterbalancing large glazed areas with delicate steel supports. A special feature was the central courtyard space around which the home wraps. However, the configuration of window joinery and poor detailing and finishing had masked the strength of the original concept.

The design aim of the architects was to simplify the building as much as possible and to break down the divisions between the spaces, and between interior and exterior. Opening the house to natural light is fundamental to the design response. The work reveals and responds to the original building rather than seeking to transform or negate it.

A primary design decision was to create a new stairwell in the existing central hallway, which allowed a direct spatial and visual link between the two levels of the house. This simple device created a sense of volume and achieved a much stronger flow from the entry down to the courtyard and other lower floor areas.

Photography Patrick Reynolds

A number of walls were removed from the living areas to create one large informal space that opens up to both the panoramic beach outlook and also the intimacy of the central courtyard. Minimalist detailing throughout the house gives the various spaces a sense of unity and expansiveness. New joinery openings to both the upper and lower level have maximised the connection to the garden from all rooms of the house. White oiled oak, weathered timber decking and white rendered walls now give a classic seaside feel to this modernist home.

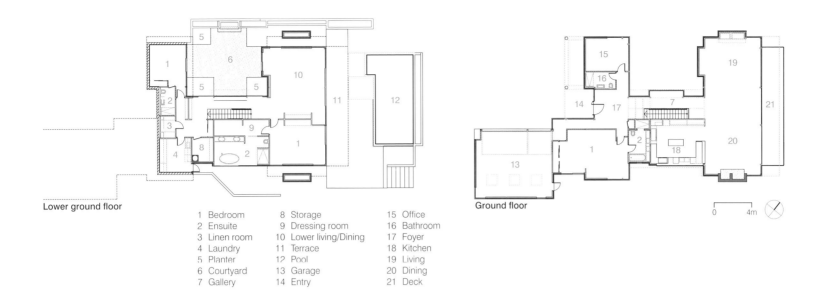

Lower ground floor

Ground floor

1 Bedroom
2 Ensuite
3 Linen room
4 Laundry
5 Planter
6 Courtyard
7 Gallery

8 Storage
9 Dressing room
10 Lower living/Dining
11 Terrace
12 Pool
13 Garage
14 Entry

15 Office
16 Bathroom
17 Foyer
18 Kitchen
19 Living
20 Dining
21 Deck

0   4m

Paul+O Architects

THE WILDERNESS
Suffolk, United Kingdom

The Wilderness sets a precedent for the new English country house in the 21st century. Sitting modestly in a clearing of a wood, its sculptural asymmetrical form brings a restrained grandeur to the picturesque setting.

The house combines traditional materials with modern detailing and construction methods. The asymmetrical volumetric massing with large cantilevers is achieved with a steel structure. Traditional and local materials, including oak and flint, and a warm grey render are used to harmonise the house with its woodland setting.

The existing grid of the site, formed by rides and hedgerows, generated a cruciform plan, which exploits aspect and shelter and opens up all elevations to the surrounding landscape. The ground-floor elevations of the house are largely transparent, dissolving the boundary between inside and out and making one feel surrounded by the landscape. The first-floor overhang is a contemporary interpretation of the traditional Suffolk medieval timber-framed house, with its projected upper storeys.

Photography Fernando Guerra

The approach to the landscaping has been to preserve and enhance the existing soft and untamed qualities of the existing woodland, so as to provide a contrast with the precise architecture of the house. The garden has been enriched with trees, shrubs and perennials native to the area, and contemporary sculptures and water features have been integrated into the woodland setting.

Ground floor

First floor

1 Pool
2 Storage
3 Plant room
4 Garage
5 Boot room
6 Laundry
7 Back hall
8 Kitchen/Dining
9 Living
10 Entrance hall
11 Library
12 Studio
13 Bedroom
14 Bathroom
15 Shower room
16 Dressing room
17 Library

clavienrossier Architectes

TRANSFORMATION IN CHARRAT
Charrat, Switzerland

Situated away from a small village in the middle of the Swiss Alps, this 19th-century property included an adjacent barn. The total volume being too large and too costly to be renewed in its entirety, only what was useful for the project was kept – cellars, the first floor and half of the second floor – while the rest was demolished in order to accommodate the new design. The existing building had no special qualities apart from the thick stone walls hidden by external plaster cement. The double-sided pitched roof was too low to allow views to the surrounding landscape from the garret floor. The existing windows were small, and a large part of the volume was blind, with half the building being used as a barn.

From the remains of the original building was created an ensemble that communicates with the surrounding vineyards, stone walls and the Alps. The strong contrast between the original and new structure is intentional. Clean geometric lines are juxtaposed with existing, rough old stone walls. Volumes of concrete tinted a stone-like colour replace the double-sided roof and the transformed area.

Photography Roger Frei

Both the new concrete volumes sit atop the existing 60-centimetre-wide wall (80 centimetres when insulation and lining is added). The idea of the sloped walls was thus conceived as a way to erase, at least visually, the thickness of the wall; to open outwards while maintaining the solidity of the existing structure.

The original building's small, vertical openings were kept to accentuate the contrast with the transformed upper level's large, horizontal windows that frame the landscape. There are no corridors and interior walls do not touch the façade, creating a sense of openness and giving each room a transversal view onto the landscape.

1 Entrance
2 Cellar
3 Laundry
4 Carnotzet (wine-tasting area)
5 Technical room
6 Living room

7 Kitchen
8 Bathroom
9 Master bedroom
10 Terrace
11 Internet/Ironing
12 Bedroom

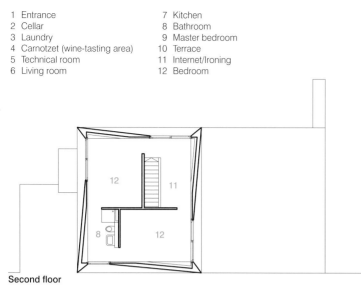

Second floor

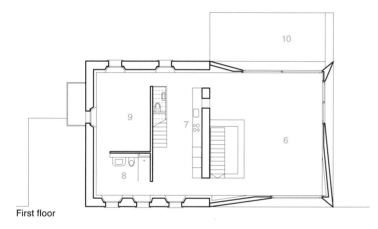

First floor

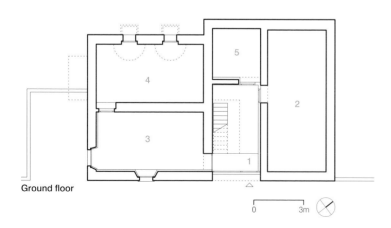

Ground floor

0   3m

123DV Architects

VILLA DALÍ
The Hague, The Netherlands

The owners of Villa Dalí had something very specific in mind when they approached the architects. They wanted a very personal house that reflected their love of the ocean and passion for art and sculpture, in particular the work of Salvador Dalí. Pictures of old Spanish architecture were also used for inspiration during the initial design discussions.

The owners were fascinated by the closed white stucco façades and metal fences in Jugendstil, or Art Noveau, design. So the challenge was to combine in one villa the beautiful Jugendstil forms, the closed façades, the treasures of the diving world and the unique works of the artist Dalí.

Photography Christiaan de Bruijne

For the design of the house the architects made use of the Paranoiac-critical method by Salvador Dalí (creating optical illusions). The result is a cylindrical white stucco main building with a nautilus spiral structure inside – representing the world of diving. The closed façade facing the street represents so-called 'Spanish' architecture with a blown-up Jugendstil pattern in the 6-metre wooden panel as the entrance. In the centre of the house is a double-storey cylindrical space. The furniture has also been custom designed, and traces of Dalí's fluid watch art can be found in its design.

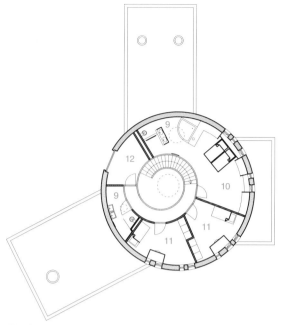

First floor

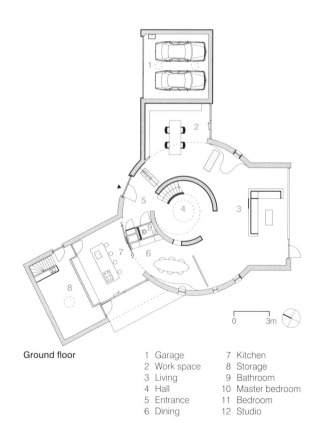

Ground floor

1	Garage	7	Kitchen
2	Work space	8	Storage
3	Living	9	Bathroom
4	Hall	10	Master bedroom
5	Entrance	11	Bedroom
6	Dining	12	Studio

Thomas Oppelt, Paddle Creek Design

VILLA DEL CIELO
Las Vegas, Nevada, USA

Villa del Cielo offers the finest amenities of new construction while capturing the timeless charm and Old World ambience of a European village. A main two-storey villa plus four private and beautifully-appointed casitas look as if they have taken centuries to perfect. Three casitas serve guests and the fourth functions as a private office and library.

Owner and Designer, Lori Venners of LVI Design, envisioned a home that lived and looked old — warm, comfortable and inviting. Teamed with Texas architect Thomas Oppelt of Paddle Creek Design and builder Greg Kaffka, the vision came to life.

Photography Synergy Sotheby's International Realty

The compound boasts incredible attention to detail and features authentic and reclaimed materials from Europe, Ecuador and Mexico. The driveway is historic reclaimed sandstone cobblestone from Western Europe. The Spanish roof is two-piece clay tile imported from Spain, installed with a blend of colours to establish an authentic look of moss and natural stains. The hardwood flooring used is a combination of reclaimed and hand-scraped Austrian ash, larch and spruce. Other reclaimed materials include cabinetry, beams, fireplace materials, and terracotta flooring imported from Southern France. The exterior and dining room canterra stone was hand-quarried and imported from Tlaquepaque, Mexico. Custom carvings and hand-painted murals add an artistic touch of elegance.

Property is Exclusively Marketed by Gene Northup, Synergy Sotheby's International Realty

1 Covered deck
2 Sitting room
3 Master wardrobe
4 Office
5 Master bedroom
6 Bathroom
7 Sauna
8 Casita
9 Casita bathroom
10 Mechanical room
11 Bedroom
12 Balcony
13 Covered porch
14 Gathering room
15 Cabana
16 Storage
17 Informal dining
18 Kitchen
19 Butler's pantry
20 Entry
21 Dining
22 Hall
23 Media room
24 Mudroom
25 Laundry
26 Garage

Ground floor

First floor

Zecc Architecten

VILLA IN THE WOODS
Soest, The Netherlands

Amid rough pine trees, in a sloping area between forest and dunes, Villa in the Woods appears like a rock breaking through the ground. The sculptural building interacts with its natural surrounds, 'pushing' out certain volumes into the landscape. Terraces are configured in such a way that, instead of being part of the garden design, they are transformed into an extension of the residence.

There is also a strong dialogue between building and landscape through the use of materials. The stony façade anchors the villa to the ground while the pinewood sections of the exterior directly reference the surrounding pine forest. The combination of form and material becomes an abstract response to the context of the landscape.

An important theme in the villa is the spatiality between the three floors. A void runs from the lower ground to the first floor, connecting all three levels. Parapets and stairs run smoothly through the void, creating a sculptural connection between the three floors.

Photography Cornbread Works

Walking through the house, one is continually surprised by the different views of the landscape. In every room the dialogue between building and landscape, and man and nature, is central. Sight lines from the front door further strengthen the relationship between the villa and the garden on three levels.

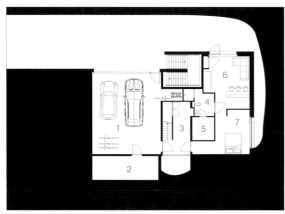

Lower ground floor

Ground floor

First floor

1 Garage	6 Guestroom	11 Dog kennel
2 Storage	7 Bedroom	12 Kitchen/Dining
3 Hall	8 Living	13 Walk-in-robe
4 Bathroom	9 Study	
5 Sauna	10 WC	

BBP Architects

WARRANDYTE RESIDENCE
Warrandyte, Victoria, Australia

This large residence, located in a cleared bush setting, was designed to engage with both the rural context of its surroundings and the Yarra River, which flows along the northeastern boundary of the property.

Contemporary in its execution, the residence consists of two wings – one functioning as a bedroom wing, while the other serves as the primary living wing. The two 'parts' of the building intersect to form an entrance vestibule that gives the house a central focus while providing usable space with 'outdoor qualities'.

The two wings also connect via two stone wall 'spines' that interface at the entrance of the residence. This space is designed to 'blur' the boundaries between outside and inside, bringing indoors the quality and the materiality of the residence and the site.

Photography Robert Hamer

The garage, which also ties in at this point, becomes the 'shed', attached to the side of the house. A timber box forming part of this shed serves as a home office looking out onto a sheltered courtyard that also opens up from the kitchen area. This 'wraps' into the entrance hall and is accentuated by a rich red stain that runs internally and externally.

The house is single storey and consists primarily of two volumes with low skillion roofs. Interior spaces are sculpted with these roof forms forming opening clerestory windows. Louvres set into these clerestories provide natural ventilation and control natural light levels entering the house. The skillions overhang the building to protect it from the summer sun while allowing the lower winter sun to penetrate the building.

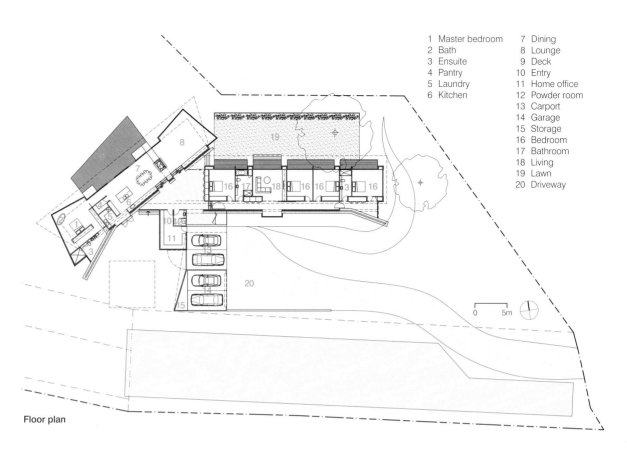

1 Master bedroom
2 Bath
3 Ensuite
4 Pantry
5 Laundry
6 Kitchen
7 Dining
8 Lounge
9 Deck
10 Entry
11 Home office
12 Powder room
13 Carport
14 Garage
15 Storage
16 Bedroom
17 Bathroom
18 Living
19 Lawn
20 Driveway

Floor plan

nervegna reed architecture + ph architects

WHITE HOUSE
Prahran, Victoria, Australia

The client, an art gallery director, asked for a contemporary home on a narrow inner-city allotment. The house was to have two bedrooms plus an extra study – to be used as accommodation for visiting artists – and a private subterranean gallery.

The house extends over three levels — the entry is located on the middle (ground) level, where all the living spaces flow around a courtyard, which is a slice of a circle. The dispersed placement of objects, materials and functions on this level works much like the layout of a pinball machine, each surface hinting at a multitude of possible routes that one could take through the building, sometimes encouraging a certain movement, sometimes not.

Photography John Gollings

The front study with adjoining bathroom is for visiting artists. Downstairs is a basement gallery, indirectly lit by a concrete light shaft/skylight that also functions as a seat and a sculpture podium.

The house works a bit like a Rorschach test, enabling people to read into it what they like. For example, the front façade might appear as a virtual '?', or the number '2'.

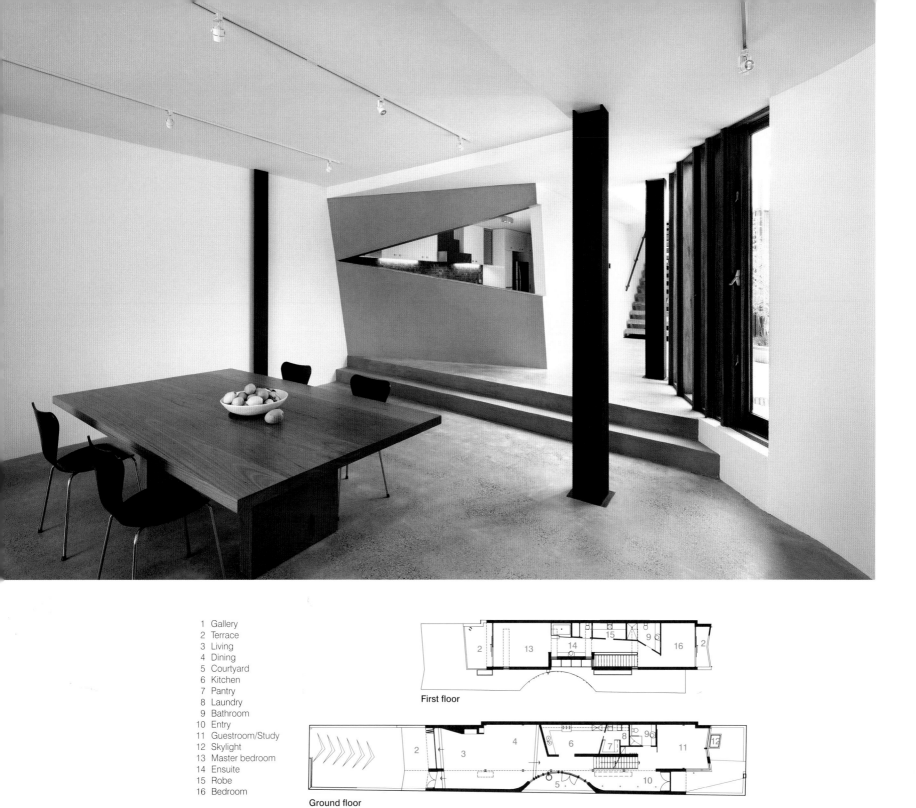

1 Gallery
2 Terrace
3 Living
4 Dining
5 Courtyard
6 Kitchen
7 Pantry
8 Laundry
9 Bathroom
10 Entry
11 Guestroom/Study
12 Skylight
13 Master bedroom
14 Ensuite
15 Robe
16 Bedroom

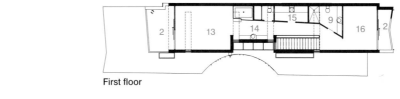

First floor

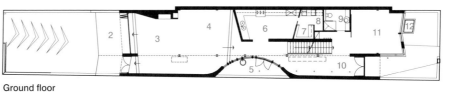

Ground floor

Lower ground floor

Stanic Harding

WOOLLAHRA HOUSE
Woollahra, New South Wales, Australia

Located on a ridge overlooking Cooper Park, the Woollahra House is one of a row of detached Federation houses built in 1901. The frontages are mostly intact, however the rear of the properties facing north are diverse in both character and quality. The quality of the renovation done to this house in the 1970s was so poor that only the front street-facing room and street façade were retained.

The project involved the complete removal of all other structure and the excavation of a new complete floor level under the existing street entry level, including a pool. The street frontage had to be restored, so the architects endeavored to create a contrasting contemporary rear façade that addressed the northern aspect and the Park. The edge treatment of the new rear balcony literally frames these views.

Photography Steve Back

The small scale of the footprint resulted in the need for careful spatial connects both horizontally and vertically to extend the available space. A new slatted light courtyard replaces the existing front terrace. Floor level changes, joinery elements and ceiling treatments create and conceal spaces.

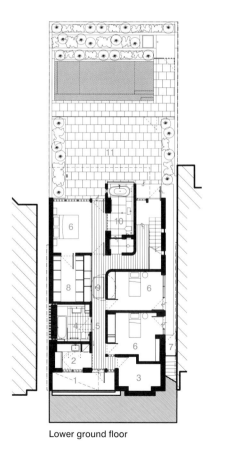

Lower ground floor

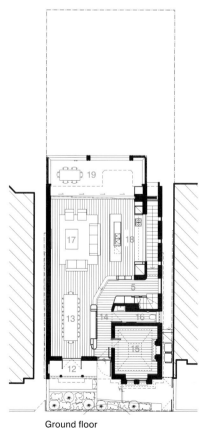

Ground floor

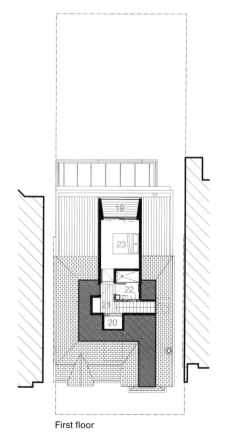

First floor

1 Courtyard
2 Laundry
3 Storage/Plant room
4 Bathroom
5 Hall
6 Bedroom
7 Garden storage
8 Walk-in-robe
9 Cellar
10 Ensuite
11 Terrace
12 Verandah
13 Dining
14 Entry
15 Study
16 Guest WC
17 Living
18 Kitchen
19 Deck
20 Void
21 Landing
22 Attic bathroom
23 Attic bedroom

0   3m

WOVEN NEST

London, United Kingdom

The Woven Nest carefully slots between buildings and sight lines, and wraps built-in furniture into every available surface. Both plan and Planning constraints generated a complex series of intertwining spaces, enlivened by light and interconnectivity.

The massing was generated from the view-lines along the High Street below, tucked carefully out of sight to achieve planning permission for a new storey, with front outdoor space hidden within the row of listed buildings.

The house assembles around the central open stairs, its timber strands growing upwards towards the light and unleashing delicate tendrils to frame each step, a single thin metallic line dancing across their lines to offer the lightest of additional support to the hands that seek it. To the right, spaces sneak into the stairs – as bathroom storage below or the underside of the desk above – while to the right the open treads fan and splay into a generous array of surfaces for the living room. Their lower steps support a seat and soft-spot, while their upper elements flow around the sitter with a sea of books and shelves.

Photography Christoph Bolten and Atmos Studios

Upstairs, the stair-tree verticals curl into architraves and continue into rooms either side of the eyelid to the sky above. Their lines flow to form a desk and shelving unit in the study, wrapping around to welcome the unfolding sheaves of floor plank that conceal a bed within the floor-depth.

The house is unified by a single curl of complex in-built furniture, bridging inside and out, closed and open, his and hers and anyone else's in its careful compaction of storage and use and its careful alignment of the body within spaces and the eye towards sky.

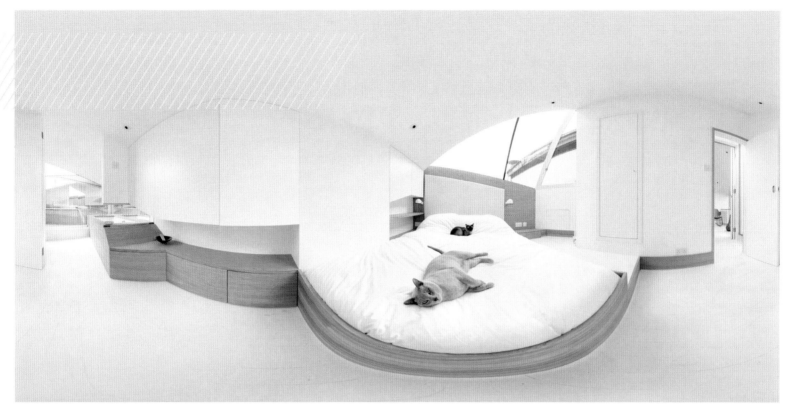

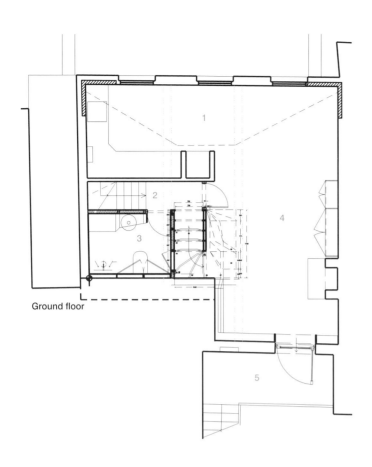

Ground floor

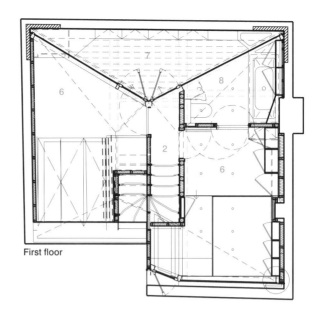

First floor

1 Kitchen
2 Hall
3 Shower room
4 Living
5 Balcony
6 Bedroom
7 Terrace
8 Bathroom

INDEX OF ARCHITECTS